Hyperrel[...] to GRACE

Thomas Rylen

ISBN 978-1-68570-651-7 (paperback)
ISBN 978-1-68570-652-4 (digital)

Christian Faith Publishing
832 Park Avenue
Meadville, PA 16335
www.christianfaithpublishing.com

Printed in the United States of America

I dedicate this book to my loving parents of 62 years of marriage. I also dedicate this book to all who are facing what seems to be insurmountable challenges or discouragement in life's path. You have it in you to be an overcomer. Jesus Loves You today. And he teaches us how to overcome through his unending grace (unearned, undeserved, unmerited favor). Enjoy this true story and harrowing mental journey that eventually took me to that place of amazing grace and rest. God Bless You!

Introduction

I have been through many challenging mental thoughts that took me to places I never intended to go. In that journey, I learned God was there all along, trying to reach me with his still small voice of peace and comfort, but my mind was overoccupied with hyperreligious thoughts. I went from having a great engineering job to living off of the streets to being admitted to a mental institution. My journey in a world of hyperreligiosity began with small red flags in my thoughts that I couldn't recognize at the time. As extreme as the story I am about to tell, believe it or not, I wouldn't take it back because it brought me to a place of God's grace, and I have learned so much.

There is an easier way than what I went through, so don't be discouraged. If we simply believe what Jesus did for us at the cross and put our trust in him, he imparts his grace, which is unearned, undeserved, unmerited favor. He wants you to have his wisdom to avoid the pitfalls I went through. I am about to take you on a journey that led to a pit of mental illness, but God was not done with me. I am a happy soul today and back on my feet.

I encourage you to give this book a read. I believe you might find it humorous, sad, bewildering, or encouraging and realize that the end of your story has not yet been written, and God has amazing plans for your life and a happy ending. This story may not be anything like you have heard or imagined, and you may find it kind of crazy. I believe it still has value and is worth telling. To protect identities, names of people have been altered. Thank you again for picking up this book.

1

The Hyperreligious Working Man

Beep, beep, beep. There it goes again. My enemy and friend. My graceful alarm that lets me know it's time to pull up my bootstraps for the day and tend to work while being on my secret mission for God. I hear the black and white cats clawing at my door.

It's time for their morning meal, and they are letting me have it with their opinion on the matter. *Meow, meow, meow.* The white cat, Sam, claws her way at black Max to get to the bowls first, even though they each have their own bowl. I quickly scramble into the claw-foot bathtub to take my half shower, half bath. "Lord, let me be light to others at work today," I pray. "Shine through me. Is it the day to give the great prophecy?"

My adventure into hyperreligiosity began with seeing a TV preacher promise me blessings for money. I was hooked. *God, you owe me*, I thought as I made out that first $1,000 check. But something in me didn't quite believe. It was almost like I had a relationship with the true God and a delusion-based God in my imagination. The one in my imagination was going to make me rich and save me through good works or at least give me a decent life on earth. "Call in now. Go to your phone. Don't let this window leave you for greater things," said the man in a shiny suit on TV.

Give it Thomas. Give it Thomas. Give it Thomas, said the voice in my head that I thought was God. A rush of adrenaline, and then I ran to the phone to give my pledge. I was going to be rich. This was the big seed I was sowing. The next day, that adrenaline pumped as I threw the check in the mailbox. This would be a pattern for a number of years in my life. I don't doubt much of it was for good to support the gospel, but some of my motives and push to do it came from my ill mind that thought of God as a big man with white flowing beard, distributing me treats from heaven's vending machine.

My hyperreligiosity kicked in high mode. I read a book on making your house "holy," so I gathered up all worldly things like alcohol, cigars, humidor, two hundred plus CDs, and whatever seemed too carnal and worldly, and I ruined them. I felt like as long as I was doing these holy acts for God that he would save me. I thought somehow, I was a super-special follower of God. After every sermon preached at my church, I felt like I must be a super follower and give into the basket. Besides, other less enthusiastic followers were watching me, and I didn't want to be the one not to give on cue. I was doing my good deeds. More shows would be on the TV, and off I would be with my $1,000 checks to various TV speakers, believing for my great riches since I was doing what they said. As long as I tithed, gave thousands of dollars to causes, then God and I "were good" with each other, and we would have a partnership, so to speak. I give to him, and I would be on his good side with the saints.

One day in my kitchen, while listening to preachers on the TV, I thought I heard from God in my mind, *One day, you will have to give a prophecy to those at your work by standing up on your desk and belting out to all the sinners like John the Baptist did.* I thought, *God, if this is you and this is true, I'll do it, but you are going to have to make me drunk on the Holy Spirit. I'm going to have to be really out of it to do that for you.*

What was I thinking? Did I really think God wanted me to stand on my desk and prophesy? This question would be the tipping point to a life of mental disorders that were not insurmountable but certainly a force to be reckoned with. I didn't know I had a mental illness at this point, but it would have served me well if I would have known and sought psychological help at this point or not soon after. So every day that I would go to work, I would be thinking, *Let me pray and be ready, but please, God, don't make me prophesy today.* The day would come and go, and relief would hit me as I headed home. I don't have to embarrass myself today. Great.

It was a foggy day out with a haze over the seawall. I walked the beach that morning and heard another religious order in my imagination that I thought was from God. *From now on, you need to carry your Bible to work, not in its case or anything. Just boldly carry it with its golden sides flashing so people can see. You are a man of God, and the world needs to know.* Or whatever other logic my mind came up with won over, but only after a few days of resisting it.

At this point in my life, I thought that my thoughts were God's thoughts for me and that I had to obey every one of them if I wanted to be his special child going to heaven. I flew to Chicago for a business trip with my Bible in hand. I was a man of religion and wanted the world to see it. *Look at me. God and I are cool.* I was sitting next to a Jewish passenger, and we got into some interesting conversations on the plane about the Old Testament.

As I ventured around Libertyville, Illinois, in my older sister's car, the thoughts kept plaguing me on how I will be that Bible boy who carries his Bible around work. What was worse is I felt like a bad person that whole weekend on the business family trip, and I know now that this was early signs of psychosis, a form of mental illness. I thought God was mad at me and that I had better carry that Bible around when I got back to work in Galveston, Texas, or else I wasn't doing what the Spirit of God wanted. I realize now I was simply caught up in hyperreligiosity.

I flew back to Galveston, stewing over my spiritual state, trying to read my religious books to see what I was supposed to do next. Ever since giving the big checks to ministries on television, I thought I was some big shot in God's kingdom who needed to constantly be doing something ultrareligious to keep this ultragodly stance. Much of it was rooted in subliminal or subconscious pride and adventure of my own mental creation.

I was on my way to work wearing the usual long-sleeved polo and dress slacks with fresh polished dress shoes. I had my big black Bible with me, and today would be the day I showed it off. It was the middle of the week, and the island I lived on was given warning of a hurricane about five days out. I was worried a little about carrying the Bible around. Was it necessary? What would people think? I felt trapped between my business life and my ultraspiritual life. The lines were blurred on what I should do.

There was all this talk in churches and TV ministries about living your faith out loud, but a misunderstanding of some of what that really means. It's not about how big your Bible is, how much you give, how many ministries you are in, or how many biblical colloquialisms you use in front of coworkers. I had the religion and zeal down in my life but not the deeper understanding of Christlikeness and pointing to Jesus, not just a bunch of religion.

Back to the Bible-carrying story. I was sitting in my car, my heart pumping, and then I just thought of this song: "No matter what that weapon is, I want you to know that I win!" I played that in my head as I bolted to the front of the building with my Bible. I left my Bible in my cubicle throughout the day. And at the end of day, I carried it back to my car for passersby to see. I felt a high, naturally, because I challenged my fear. From this day forward, my life would become about being a religious adrenaline junkie. The problem is that religion is not a game, and it's not about adrenaline. God works by love. I would eventually figure this out while more aware of my mental illness later in life.

I was sitting in my cubicle, working on a Saturday, and this fellow came up to me and asked for a ride home. He didn't know me, but he guessed I might be a cordial employee and help, and I did. About a week later, he was gravely affected by the hurricane. I helped him clean out his apartment, and we tried to salvage what good things we could.

He took a liking to me as a person and would come by my cubicle every couple of days to talk. We would talk about God and religion. I think at the time, I was too much of a baby believer in Jesus to give him strong cases for the Christian life. But I was also learning, in spite of my illness, more about the love of God. God wants us to love first, and if he opens the door, talk about his goodness and plan of salvation for us. It took me a while to discover how to talk about God in a more effective way. Maybe I will get to that later in the book.

I was driving down my alley, coming home from a business trip. It was dark out, and I saw this Black woman hanging out near my home, looking lost. I asked her if I could help her, and she asked for a beer. I told her I could give her some food. I had just bought a bag full of mini burgers and decided to give them to her. She had basically recently come off the streets and was getting help by the city with housing. She lived a few homes over, right off the alley. Her alley apartment was empty, except for a chair. She was sleeping off of the carpet. I thought that I couldn't just let this person live like this, so I started to give her extra furniture from my home—a bed from my spare bedroom, a bookshelf and extra books, a vanity, and little extras that I thought might help. I told her that I would be going to church the next morning and invited her to go with me.

I was sitting at my desk, preparing the cost estimates for the Port of Galveston. We would be meeting with them at their building in a few hours.

I had this thought that I should bring my Bible to the meeting but thought also that it would be out of place. I ended up bringing it in its case but left it in the government truck we drove up in. My fear won out in this case, though I still think it was part of my hyperreligiosity that thought about bringing it in the first place.

A similar thing happened one day as I was supposed to go to this mini meeting at a coworker's desk, and something told me to bring the Bible to her desk. Once again, I caved and didn't follow through with this, though I felt partly bad about myself for not doing this.

Every day at lunch, I would carry my big Bible to the cafeteria for everyone to see. *Look at me*, I thought. Part of me was thinking kind of like a Pharisee. I know now that I needed to grow more in the love of God, that he should get the glory for what we do. If we are moved by our looks and not Christ, that is not what God wants. If you carry your Bible around, I'm not against that. As long as your faith is rooted in Jesus alone, it's what you want to do from your heart and not your self-righteousness.

Another business trip came up where I was going to a risk management course for dams. While I was there, my hyperreligious mind brought back the memory of giving the prophecy like John the Baptist. Something told me that I needed to give it while on the trip to the people in the class I was taking. I fought this thought tooth and nail and felt rather depressed and oppressed the entire business trip. I bought a Christian book and also browsed through a book about Mother Teresa in the store. I was trying to get my mind off the prophecy because my thoughts also told me that I would have to give it to my coworkers when I got back to Galveston. I was severely anxious and religiously schizophrenic, though I didn't know this at the time.

Monday, while back at the office, I went on a little field trip to a dam site in Houston called Addicks and Barker Dams. In my spare time, when people weren't watching, I would cry out to God in prayer, "Please deliver me from giving this prophecy. Nevertheless, not my will, but yours be done." I was trapped and didn't know how to get the prophecy thoughts out of my head. Because I told God I would do it several years back while in my home, I felt like a bad person and maybe even on the way to hell if I didn't follow through.

My entire system of thought at the time is that you keep every promise to God, your vows, and if you don't, you're hell bound. I didn't have a revelation of his grace and the courage just to completely cast the care on him and let go of it. But my day was coming. After I got back from work, I met up with my parents who were staying the night in Galveston. We visited in a hotel room, and my mother encouraged me to follow the path God had for me in life. "Go to Africa if needed," she said.

The next morning, I decided enough was enough with the prophecy thoughts, so I put on my best suit, polished my shoes, and headed to work. At about 9:00 a.m., I first walked into a meeting with my big Bible. I needed to hype myself up for the prophecy. I then left the meeting after about ten minutes, walked to my desk on the second floor of the building, stood up, and said, "Thus saith the Lord, repent!" I didn't scream it but said it in a comfortable room voice.

A guy in the cubicle next to me heard it and said, "What?"

That moment, I got down from my desk and decided to head straight to my boss's office to resign. I knew immediately that the best thing for me to do was resign instead of further embarrassing myself and getting in trouble for being unruly. She wasn't there, so I went to her boss. "Listen, Adam, I've been doing some thinking, and I think it's best if I put my notice in. I will be leaving today," I said.

Then Adam said, "Are you sure, Thomas? We have put too much pressure on you. In the regular army, we give breaks for your situation." We were in the US Army Corps of Engineers, a civilian side of the army. "Maybe we could work something out," said Adam.

This would have been an ideal time to bring up that I have some mental issues and that with some time seeing some kind of shrink, I could recover from this. But I simply did not have insight at this time into my mental illness. I had a case of hyperreligiosity, probably OCD and some psychosis, but I just didn't see it yet. After a long day of meetings and trying to summarize the different project statuses for my boss, I headed home.

While at Walmart the next day, shopping, I had this strong burning in my stomach like I didn't give the right prophecy at work and that I should also give my two weeks' notice and give them some more of my time before flat-out leaving. I called my boss and told her I could work two more weeks. She was grateful for that, but she didn't know I was also planning on giving the prophecy. So I returned to work on a Thursday, suited up in my nice navy-blue suit with shiny shoes and a tie.

I was going to give the prophecy. I prayed to God in my car, "God, I'm going to do this. If this is not your will, then I need you to stop me." God did deliver in this instance, for I was completely swamped with people coming by my desk the entire day and asking how I was doing, and something in my thoughts at this point told me the prophecy was unnecessary. The day flew by with many distractions, and I ended up not giving that prophecy from my desk.

After going home with a coworker, I decided I would not finish my two weeks' notice at work again. That job environment was just a bad trigger, and I needed a total break from the prophecy thoughts from potentially popping up again. I had struggled with that for a year and half, and enough was enough. My coworker was a very sweet gal originally from China. She let me rest at her place over the weekend, made a really good spaghetti dinner, and encouraged me with scripture.

At this point, I had my mind on seeking new ventures, such as landscaping or something completely different, not in an office where I would feel compelled to give a prophecy from my desk. Before the weekend was over, my ex-boss threw me a nice going-away party at her house with many people from the office. I was starting to feel a new freedom and release, but this would be short-lived after new religious pressures would rear their head in the months ahead. That Sunday, I made one final trip to the office to clear out my personal stuff from my desk. I was leaving for good.

2

Being a Fool for Jesus

I began to make business cards and door hangers for my new landscaping business. I would go door-to-door to try and drum up customers. Not long after I started the landscaping business, which was primarily lawn-care jobs, I had a thought that God was telling me to preach on a street corner. Day after day, the thoughts wouldn't go away, so I started to drive by this particular location at the corner of Broadway and Seawall and pray about preaching there.

Once again, this all sounds super spiritual and almost like a calling, but it was just the mental illness trying to tell me I was a special agent for God. Yes, God calls people, but he is much gentler and leaves it up to our free will to follow him, not giving overwhelming pressure-filled thoughts with the idea that if we don't act on it, we are going to hell. In my lack of insight into God's grace, I went to that corner time after time, trying to motivate myself to fulfill this preaching idea. I would dress up in my suit, go to the corner, and then chicken out and feel condemned all the time for not doing it.

One Friday, as I was at the store, I felt like the cashier was treating me like a second-class citizen, not making eye contact, and sounding indifferent. This was one of many recent incidents when dealing with other people. I felt like I was this bad person, and God was dealing with me for not fulfilling his directive to preach. After this incident with the store clerk, I broke down, went to my house, and told God while looking in the mirror that I would go to that street corner and preach.

While my workers were on a landscaping job, I suited up, brought my Bible and a milk crate to stand on, and went to that street corner. For thirty minutes, as cars would stop, I belted out Bible verses and warned people of their state without Jesus. After I left that place, I felt exhilarated, but my zeal was before the proper time and place, and it was just a personal high for doing something kind of radical.

Now that I thought I was a bona fide street preacher and feeling the high in it, which is probably not the right reason to do it, I would go to that intersection every day and preach. I didn't even really fully understand the gift of salvation and God's plan, but I was acting out on what I thought mentally was the right path. In reality, I was pushing myself too hard with the wrong motives. Nevertheless, I feel God did use what I was doing to get others' attention. In the back of my mind, there was still a mental illness that thought I must walk this perfect line with God to be saved. It would be years later that I understood his grace and love and gentleness with believers.

Once, while I was in my kitchen before going out to preach, I felt like I should be like Paul the Apostle. From what I read about Paul, he was very motivated, unconventional, and willing to do what it takes to capture the lost and bring them into the kingdom of God. I had this thought that I should put this crazy headband on with palm leaves propped up between headband and head and shout at people on the street corner to get their attention.

I dismissed this headband with palm leaves routine, but when I went back to the site where I would usually preach, I felt like the Lord wanted me to cluck like a chicken in front of everybody near the intersection. The thought of the chicken impression didn't go away. Again, I would drive to that corner and pray about it. I got into a trap with my words. I said, "Lord, if you want me to cluck like a chicken at this street corner, then I will." The thoughts plagued me for days on end.

While I was in church, filming the service on the church camera, I felt like the Lord said, "Go ahead and do the chicken, but do it like you are a kingdom child, with confidence and authority, and do it at twelve noon the next day."

I went back to that intersection, dressed up in my suit, and at exactly twelve noon, I went ballistic and started doing a chicken impression right in front of the red-light traffic. Some guy drove by and began shouting in support of this craziness. I felt a jolt of freedom after this but also felt like I should continue doing the chicken. Every time the traffic came to a red light, I would act like a chicken right in front of the cars before the light turned green.

In between religious acts for the Lord, I would take breaks. I was in my black suit and nice dress shoes. I was sitting on the bare concrete at the bottom of Seawall. I liked to chill at this little hideout when I needed a break from my escapades for the Lord. The place was near seagrass and sand, close to where one of my homeless friends hung out. There were some old dilapidated structures that once were beach hangouts in the old days where one could get souvenirs or an ice-cold beverage on a hot sunny day. This was my place to collect my thoughts and regroup. I could hide from the world and cars passing by.

My homeless friend saw me and decided to say hello. He was an interesting fellow. He had scraggly hair and a beard and looked very intent when he spoke to me, like he had trained his mind well to engage others. He gave me one of his nice rose-shaped palm-leaf figurines that he made for friends and to try to solicit funds from others. He was a very exciting soul full of stories of dreams in life he had, like moving up north on his friend's farm and doing things the old way. He had a long life.

Once a construction worker, he was now trying to make his way sleeping by seagrass and behind alleys of local buildings across the seawall. As I sat there, I could smell the fresh and salty ocean air while also hearing the daily car traffic behind me. My homeless friend was giving me a pep talk. He would tell me that I was on the A team in life. He said that the world was full of lost souls but that I was special. Was this man part of God's plan to encourage me to keep going and doing the things I was doing for the Lord?

One day, while at the intersection, while doing the chicken and also preaching, a cop showed up and told me that he was concerned for my safety. He also said I had to leave the intersection. I asked him if I needed a permit to preach, and he said yes.

I decided I would do religious acts near but not at the intersection, in the grassy triangle area nearby, and also the seawall by a McDonald's, and in my spare time, try to get a permit from the city to preach at that street corner. Sometimes I would do push-ups and jumping jacks at the grassy area in my suit. I would try to get people's attention. When strangers would ask what I was doing, I would tell them that I was on a mission for the Lord.

I was sitting in a coffee shop close to the intersection where I typically ministered. I was sitting there with my Bible and backpack, drinking my coffee, and attempting to hear from the Lord. I had this thought that I would be dancing in this grassy triangle area right next to the intersection. I believed at the time that the Lord was speaking to me through my thoughts. My thoughts told me that I would go to the grassy area (where much traffic passed by) and do a wild kind of dance very sporadically and without a single care in the world. Something told me in my mind that the police would come by and try to stop me, but I was simply to say, "I am dancing for Jesus."

And so I went there at about 6:00 p.m. I began to act like a real crazy man, dancing my feet off, jumping in the air, and putting my thumb on my nose with fingers wiggling in the air. It looked stupid. Someone actually called me stupid. Many people would honk or shout or give me a funny look. Eventually, the police came around, asking what I was doing, and I told them, "I am dancing for Jesus."

They didn't know what else to say and left me to keep dancing. I danced at this spot till about 3:00 a.m.. Many times before 3:00 a.m., I would try to figure out if I could stop doing this for the Lord, and I kept having the thought to keep dancing in faith.

I woke up the next day, and my feet were killing me. I put a lot of stress on them. I went to meet up with a friend at lunch, and he told me the rumors that had reached him about my dancing. At some point, he told me, "Don't dance the way David did."

David, the king in the Bible, at one point in his worship to the Lord, danced in his servant clothes (without the kingly garb) in public, but some people have wrongly interpreted that he danced naked. When my friend, John, told me not to dance naked, he opened a door in my mind to think I was supposed to dance like David, to go to the intersection, get naked, and dance. I kept thinking and believing that God was telling me to dance like naked David.

I would try to push the naked dancing thoughts out of my head, and my feet were very tired from the previous night's dancing. In order to keep up doing things for the Lord, I decided to do gestures kind of like a mime on the seawall. I would go to the area I once preached and danced and do these odd-looking bodily gestures. The signature gesture was standing on one leg, putting one arm out like a plane, and putting my thumb on my nose while wiggling my fingers. It looked very silly and probably comical to some.

Every morning, I would wake up and have the naked dancing thoughts in my mind, and I felt a burning in my heart about it. I kept trying to push this away. I would go out to the seawall to do the gestures. People would ask me if I was okay. I believed God wanted me to do them, so I pushed through the social awkwardness and kept doing the gestures. I would take breaks in between. On one occasion, I started to do the silly miming/gestures in front of a bar across the seawall. I was there for a number of hours. I finally left but then felt a burning sensation to return. I said, "God, I believe this is you, so I'm going to go back." I went back to that location and started to do the gestures again, and a woman from the bar came over to me to ask me what I was doing. I told her I was being a fool for Jesus. She said that her husband at the bar was depressed and losing the will to live, but my gestures gave him hope.

Now time out here. I'm not opposed to helping others in different ways, but I was pressured by my condition into the gestures, preaching, dancing, prophecy, etc. God used them for good because that's what it says in Romans 8:28, but I had a mental illness and hyperreligiosity issues that kept me doing very unconventional things that I thought God was leading me in.

The next day, the naked dancing thoughts were so strong I finally snapped and decided to leave Galveston, go live with my parents in Spring, Texas, and run from what I thought God was telling me. I was very spiritually uncomfortable at my parents' home. I felt like I had abandoned God and didn't feel right. I continued to ignore this and attempted to start a new life at my parents' home. I would go to job fairs and even got an interview in engineering. The feelings like I was wrong with God were so strong this would have been a good time to see some kind of therapist, but I just didn't have enough insight into my condition at this time, and the feelings were truly overwhelming.

One morning, while feeling like a big disappointment to God and feeling incredibly wrong for being in Spring, I cried out to God and told him I would face life again in Galveston. I would go back. In the back of my mind, I thought I might have to dance naked like David did. I told my parents I was going back on a mission to Galveston, and they were very concerned and afraid for me. My dad had a long talk with me about life and just gave me fatherly moral support.

For about eight months in Galveston, I continued to go out to the seawall to do gestures and tell people I was being foolish for the Lord. I never converted anybody but did have interesting spiritual talks with others. Some would make fun of me and some would embrace my silliness. I made a number of friends, mainly with homeless people. I eventually came to a point where I felt like God was telling me to give away everything that I owned. Before I get into this, I had cleared up the dancing naked thoughts. I prayed to God about it and felt like he was saying that was the Old Testament and telling me not to worry about it. Some of my relationship with God was legitimate like this instance, but for years, I would struggle with psychosis and confusion about what was and wasn't God's will.

Back to the "giving everything away" story. I started to donate furniture and items to the church I went to. One time, after buying food from the store, I felt like I wasn't supposed to do that and that I had disobeyed God, especially considering the coffee I bought, since that was a nonessential item. I felt like God was telling me to carry a box of books and the coffee up to the altar at church, so I obeyed this perceived command, and right before service started, I dropped off these items at the altar for all to see. The urge to give everything away kept persisting, so I kept making trips to the church to give away items. It came to a point where I thought God wanted me to give my two cats to the church.

After being overly pressured, I finally relented and drove the cats up to the church on a weekday. They couldn't accept them, of course, and even after doing this, the pressure kept growing to still give the cats to the church, say, on a Sunday right before church service. I chickened out on this, and a spiritual leader who was anticipating me coming up to the church with the cats told me to give them to the local shelter.

One day, while sitting in my living room with overwhelming thoughts about the cats, I decided enough was enough and gave them to the animal shelter. I felt bad but also felt so trapped in my spiritual delusion about possibly embarrassing myself and bringing the cats to a church service. After giving them to the shelter, the thoughts about giving the cats were still strong. I called a spiritual leader in the church to see if he could loan me money to get the cats out of the shelter. I still felt like they should go to the church. He talked me down from this with encouragement and scripture.

Eventually, the house I lived in was being foreclosed on because I wasn't making payments. I was so caught up in doing the gestures for the Lord that I failed to get a job in time to keep up with the mortgage payments. I did try to get small odd jobs, but nothing that could significantly sustain living in that home I bought when I was previously an engineer. I sold the rest of my belongings for pennies on the dollar, got out of the house, and moved to my parents' home in Spring, Texas. Right before I left my Galveston home, I felt strong feelings that I should stay. For the first time in a very long time, I reasoned with myself and convinced myself it was the right thing to do to leave, and I had help making this decision from a spiritual leader in the church.

3

A Crisis of Virility

After being at my parents' place for four months, life began to look up in general. I landed an engineering job in Houston and was attending Bible school at night at my church in La Marque, Texas. I would pray in tongues for hours while in the car on the way and back from work and on the way to Bible school at night. The gift of tongues is a supernatural language that God gives to believers where his Spirit is praying through you for things you may not know naturally. Life was running smoothly until I had some very strange thoughts again.

I was sitting at my desk at a rented home, playing Monopoly on the internet. I got up to get a cup of coffee, and this weird thought hit me. *Do people donate sexual organs?* Why would I think this? Then the next question in my head went off. *Would I be willing to donate my sexual organs?* Instead of letting these weird thoughts pass, I then said a prayer to God, "If it be thy will, so be it."

What in the world was I thinking? I began to get uneasy about it like I felt about all prior religious prayers I had prayed in the past. I began to feel trapped. But the thought didn't end there. The next thought came up. *Would I be willing to give my sexual organ in the form of an offering at the front of the church in front of everybody?* Another preposterous thought. Then I said another prayer, "If it be thy will, so be it."

Why did I pray this? The answer in my mind was simple. Anything I could think of in a religious way was a potential action that God might want of me. Little did I know this would be a trap for some time. Our words are powerful. What we agree to, we should consider carefully. Of course, Jesus would reveal later that he came to give me life and life more abundantly, as it says in John 10:10, not requiring me to perform self-sabotaging acts to my body.

I was plagued for the next week, less able to focus on the job at work, and constantly casting the care on God. "Lord, should I give my sexual organ to church at the altar?" I kind of felt like this was a big secret between me and the Lord. I think part of me was ashamed to think this way, but I was deep in religiosity. So why did I think and pray this way? Again, it goes all the way back to my giving large sums of money to televangelists years ago. I thought that as long as I was led by the Lord as I perceived that to be, then I was his and going to heaven. As long as I was following the Lord in what I believed that to be, the Devil couldn't touch me.

On the way to a church camp meeting, the thoughts of sexual-organ offering were so strong that I cried out to the Lord, "Lord, if you want me to cut myself open in front of the church and donate my sexual organs, then so be it." I felt like the spiritual climate around me was like a hornet's nest that I just stirred up. The devil was laughing at the stupidity of my prayer. Going to church started becoming a very tricky walk for me because these ridiculous thoughts that I agreed to, if it was God's will, would continually come up.

I started down another path in which every time the thoughts came up about sexual-organ donation, I would raise my hands, lift my head toward heaven, and say, "Lord, I cast this care on you." Not so much agreeing to donate my sexual organ, but giving these unbearable thoughts to God so that I could begin to get peace in the matter and keep following the Lord's Spirit to know that I am saved.

This was becoming a bit repetitive, I know. This cycle of thinking about sexual-organ donation and casting the care on God went on for about a year and a half before I was eventually admitted to a mental institution for other related religiosity problems. For now, I will fill in some other religious experiences and get to the institution experience later.

Eventually, I decided to share the thoughts with a church member at prayer time at the front of the church altar during prayer. He told me that I should have come forward with this earlier. I also shared it with a spiritual mentor of mine, and he helped me feel less stigmatized by the ridiculous reality of the dilemma I was facing.

While the sexual organ thoughts kept coming up, I was attending a two-year Bible school that I was sponsored in by a generous man. On one occasion in class, a teacher was talking about the importance of integrity on the job because you must live out your witness of God in your life in front of others. I believe this is true, but I think we still need to be more in tune to God's gentle Spirit instead of getting on a tangent about a perceived moral dilemma. Eventually, I got very religious and a bit obsessive-compulsive about my time sheet at my job.

Long story short, I went to my boss to vent about some time that she had me charge to on a project that was not accurate. I told her from now on, I would only charge exactly as the work reflected. I told her about my spreadsheet with very accurate time, and she asked whether when I was inputting time in the spreadsheet, I accounted for the time inputting time.

I told her that I charged to the project for time in which I was inputting time for, if that makes any sense. But I got anal about it and tried to refine the spreadsheet to record time on projects down to the second. This, of course, was impossible, but my overly perfectionistic and religious mind tried to pursue this. I then changed course, and I would waste time by trying to exclude time that I spent on the spreadsheet from the time sheets. I spent so much time on the spreadsheet that I was not charging a full eight hours a day to actual projects. I was spending two to three hours a day on the spreadsheet. I tried to deduct bathroom breaks, coffee breaks, and even time getting materials together, such as retrieving file folders and opening engineering programs on the computer. This overly compulsive behavior began to affect my work performance on the job, and I was eventually let go. This wasn't the only reason, but it played a part in my job performance leading to termination.

After being let go from work, I went home to the house my sister and I were sharing rent on. I began to get up late every day and then work on my résumé. I would also take very long prayerful walks at nearby park trails. I had new thoughts pop up about a past ministry I pursued in which I would do a type of miming on the seawall in Galveston to attract people to witness to about Jesus. I had thoughts that

I should do the religious miming again in parts of Houston. I thought it looked stupid, though, and didn't want to do it. But I also didn't want to let God down. Like the sexual-organ donation thoughts, I would repeatedly cast this care on God and pray for hours in tongues while walking around the park. I would also often lift my hands, look up to heaven, and cast my cares on God. Someone watching would probably wonder what in the world was going on with me.

In addition to the repetitious looking up to heaven and casting my cares on God, I started to develop a way of praying to try and fool the devil from interfering. My new routine was to talk to God in my mind about what I was going to pray and what I really meant and then say the prayer out loud after prefacing it in my thoughts first. I felt like this preparation of my prayer before saying it out loud would guard against the devil trying to use my words against me by twisting what I said. I could genuinely go to God and say, "Remember what I said I meant in my mind before praying it?"

I don't do this anymore because I have come to realize that God knows my heart and gives me his holy words in the Bible to combat against the deceitfulness of the devil. Words like "No weapon formed against me shall prosper" (Isaiah 54:17). This includes combatting against the devil regarding self-mutilation thoughts (castration and donation at altar of sex organ). Other scriptures to combat castration included "I am a living sacrifice," "I am fearfully and wonderfully made," "Jesus came to give me life and life more abundantly," which includes healing, the opposite of self-destruction. There are many scriptures I would quote to combat negative thoughts and wrongful actions.

4

Living Off the People and Walmart

Eventually, I was not able to pay rent to my sister, and I felt like I should leave. Looking back on it, I should have stayed put at my sister's and continued to pursue work to try and help out, but that's the past now. I left my sister's place and started to live out of my truck. I would stay in the Heights in Houston and eventually left there and went to a truck stop called Loves. I stayed there a couple of nights and decided to leave there.

I went to a large park in Houston and walked around praying the whole day there. I was dirty, hungry, and tired of living out of my truck. I prayed to God for food, and I felt like he was telling me to stay put by my truck in the park. Lo and behold, in about half an hour, a woman came around ministering food to those in need, and she gave me a sack lunch and encouraged me in the Lord.

Later that day, I prayed to the Lord for a shower. There was a pool at the park, and the thought crossed my mind to take a dip in the pool as a kind of bath. I went to the front desk at the pool, and they said it was free for Houston residents. I showed my ID and went in. They wanted me to take a shower in their showers first, so I did that. Another prayer answered.

Later in the day, I asked the Lord for a bed to sleep in, and the thought crossed my mind to go to the Salvation Army. I went there and stayed the night.

The next morning, I had just enough gas to drive forty miles south to my church in La Marque, Texas. I drove to the church and was confronted by a lady that said I looked tired and stressed. I told her about my living out of truck and Salvation Army in Houston, and she began to inquire of others if I could stay at their place. We came across one of my church friends and told him my story. He agreed to come let me stay at his place.

I was living on his couch and would get up every day and pray in the Spirit for an hour or so while he was at work. He gave me some work to do around the house. I would often do outdoor work and then go into prayer sessions. My life had become long prayer sessions, casting cares on God, and quoting scripture against self-mutilation. I would also go to places to apply for basic work, like coffee shops. For some reason, after time, I started to feel uneasy about living with my friend Patrick. Looking back on it now, I realize I was overly religious, and I probably should have let those feelings go and stay there with Patrick while trying to rebuild my life.

I eventually left Patrick's place about the time my retirement funds (I cashed in early) came in the mail. I had about two to three weeks' worth of motel living. During that time, I prayed a lot and went on small road trips in the area near my church in La Marque, Texas. The money eventually ran out, and I headed to the house of another friend, Jim. Jim and his family let me stay about a week, then they said I had to leave. I left Jim's and ended up at a park about twenty miles away. There I got some water and spent the day thinking and praying about where to go next.

Later that night, I headed to a mall about two miles from church. I slept in my truck and was awoken late at night by a police officer who said I couldn't stay there. I asked him if he knew of a place I could park, and he indicated that the Walmart about a half mile away allowed for campers. I drove to the

Walmart and slept the night in my truck. This would become my hangout for a number of months.

I can remember when I was living out of my truck in the Walmart parking lot in Texas City, Texas, that the Lord was with me. I remember getting up every morning and confessing God's promises over me for health, a sound mind, and provision. I was in an awkward place. I had been on the run spiritually from the thought that I would have to castrate myself and give an offering of myself in front of the church. Yes, the thoughts were still with me. Again, some scriptures that I would confess were, "No weapon formed against me shall prosper, and every tongue that comes against me shall be condemned;" or "I am fearfully and wonderfully made;" or "I am a living sacrifice before God;" or "I have the mind of Christ;" or "God thinks many precious thoughts towards me like the number of sand particles;" and more. My routine would be to begin praising God when I woke up, to take a walk to the other end of the parking lot and pray in the Spirit, pray in the natural under-standing, and quote God's Word to myself.

I went through a phase where I felt it was important to know God was feeding me meals by faith and faith only. I was a bit off on my theology by many times rejecting food and provision. There were some supernatural prayers answered where I would find money. One time, I was praying for dinner, and a $20 bill came flying across the parking lot. On other occasions, I received $20 and $100 bills from others. I was living poor out of my truck, relying on asking others for money to put gas in my vehicle. Sometimes I would walk two miles to church from the Walmart parking lot. Many times, I was plagued with various strange thoughts, including the thought of castration. I would simply lift up my hands to heaven and say, "Lord, I cast these cares on you." I was later diagnosed with OCD and schizophrenia, but I will get to that later.

I started to get real cold in my truck as winter season came on, so I bummed some change from Walmart shoppers and, around Thanksgiving week, headed to the Salvation Army in Galveston. That night, I started to make conversation with random roommates. We talked about the things of God and faith. The next morning, I drove three guys to a special breakfast called the hobo breakfast on Saturday mornings in Galveston near Twentieth Street and Winnie Street. I started to not trust two of the guys and told them I couldn't drive them anymore. We all walked about a block to the breakfast. It became a weekend routine to go to the breakfast, get toiletries, more clothes, and hear the Word of God while we filled our bellies with wholesome food.

While I was staying at the Salvation Army, I would converse with this one girl that I sensed came from a background of witchcraft. I told her that she could get free from the generational iniquity that was passed down in her family. She got really defensive and told me to not bring up her family. I would notice that every time I saw her around town or at the Salvation Army, she would come up to me and pat me on the back and say hello. As weird as this sounds, I feel like she was doing some kind of spiritual transfer in the form of witchcraft. I was probably off in my theology.

Later, she got offended by something else I said, and she told me she was not a bad person. After this, things got weird at the Salvation Army. I think she made some kind of deal with this other guy in the dark arts. This one guy would try to have different people corner me while he would get really close and look them in the eye. I sensed he was up to something in the form of witchcraft, so I began to witness about God and the Gospel to everyone he tried to do his magic with on me. It was my own strategy of interfering with his work. I could see he would get to a point of frustration that the things he was trying were not working. I still left the Salvation Army to get away from this guy and the negative atmosphere.

I headed back to Walmart fifteen miles north and stayed there again. A few weeks later, I thought I would try Galveston again. When I got back, the previous guy in witchcraft was there with one of his new friends, who had tattoos covering his entire body.

This man looked like an ex-convict. He was covered in tattoos and put his bed mat near mine. He would wake up in the night with this dark laugh and make jokes of how he was going to get my family in Spring. He would mockingly do religious chants around me and pray like a deranged monk. He tried to follow me out of the shelter in the morning. This was getting too creepy, so I bailed out from the situation and drove back to the Walmart parking lot in Texas City, Texas.

I lived in the Walmart parking lot for some time (three to four more months) and then got the feeling that God wanted me to preach again. I didn't want to do it, but once again, with my words, I said I would if that was what God wanted. My mental illness was getting worse. I suited up in my nice interview suit I got from college (it had been hanging up in the back cab of my truck) and brought this small file container to stand on.

I went to a street corner near Popeyes Chicken, about two miles from the church, and started belting out scripture and warnings again about the doom of those without Jesus. I did this a couple of times and would feel feelings of condemnation when I didn't go to preach. I noticed I wasn't feeling right in my mind and was not able to keep my groceries that I bought from panhandling. I felt like they didn't come from God and I should donate them to the church. So I went up to the church and donated half-eaten food items. Not long after that, I was desperate for some normalcy in my life, to not have to use Walmart's bathroom to freshen up, to not live in my truck anymore. I got some gas money from a generous person and headed seventy miles up to Spring, Texas, where my folks live.

5

The Homeless
Street Preacher

I was down to 130 pounds. To no fault of my parents, I had a lack of peace staying at their home, so when they were out, I drove off about two miles down the road and stayed the next night in my truck. When I was without anything to do, just sitting there in my truck, I thought maybe God would have me to preach. Also, I felt like preaching was a way to escape the many thoughts plaguing my mind at the time.

I went to a street corner near an AutoZone and belted out scripture and people's doom without Jesus. Later that night, I was tired of the area I was in (parked near a business complex) and decided to drive south on what little gas I had. I was getting low on gas, so I stopped in a parking lot off Farm to Market Road 1960 in an area that seemed kind of dangerous. Every day, I would go out near the highway bridge intersection and spend some time preaching. There were other hobos around panhandling for money. Some of them took a liking to me and gave of their food supply. Later one evening, after eating a meal from a hobo, I felt like I wasn't supposed to eat it, so I forced myself to gag it up. After about a week in that area of Houston, once again, I panhandled money for gas and headed to my parents.

This would be short-lived. After telling them I was going to leave again, they gave me a big bag of food and a hundred dollars. I would spend the night in random parking lots at different businesses and continue with my long prayers filled with scripture to try and gain some hope about going forward in life. I started to develop obsessive-compulsive disorder about walking on other peoples' property. If I just barely touched the edge of their property, I would go to the manager of the business and apologize for being on their property. One day, while in a shopping center, I went door-to-door to each business to apologize. This was getting overwhelming, so I bailed from this area in Spring, drove south toward Houston, and parked my truck on the side of the road near an industrial complex.

I was hot in my truck and thirsty. I was low on gas, so this would be my spot for a while. I needed water badly. I decided to suit up in my $500 navy blue suit from Jos. A. Bank that I got back in college. I put on my nice dress shoes. I was on a mission for God. I would pray to him for gas, water, food, and the right place to preach or witness to the lost one-on-one. All this was good, but it was like an escape from my homeless situation and from constantly being on the run to find a place to settle and get victory over delusional thoughts.

On my second or third day being in this area, I decided I needed a break from the preaching and was getting a little tired of living out of my truck. I decided I would pack up a backpack with important papers, a book, an outfit of clothing, and offerings I wanted to give to church next time I was there, and head to the Salvation Army about fifteen miles into Houston. I was ditching my truck. As I was about a mile from the truck, I passed by this Popeyes Chicken. I barely stepped foot on the pavement of the Popeyes parking lot and felt like I should apologize to the manager for being on his property illegally. Though I was only passing by, and this was no big deal, my mind made it out to be a big deal and of religious significance.

I went in and asked for the manager and apologized to him for being on his property illegally. After

I left here, I then began to believe I should go back and show him my ID and apologize again. Before I could make sense out of this, I had a thought that I should show him all my credentials (my bag had a birth certificate and other papers of significance) and strip down naked for him. Basically, the logic was that I would be offering myself in total innocence to him and seeking his forgiveness. I know this is twisted stuff. I couldn't get the thought out of my head, so I decided to get rid of most of my credentials, including my birth certificate and a bunch of old papers and a trophy and award I got from Bible college by throwing these things down the city drain. I held on to my driver's license, social security card, and the offerings for church. I was basically trying to simplify what I had and get out of the area to avoid being around Popeyes and feeling delusional religious conviction to disrobe there.

The thoughts were strong in my mind. I made it about a mile down the road when something told me to return to the area. I believe it was some additional church offering I needed to get from my truck. So I came back, and I ran into a man that I met a day earlier. He blessed me with some pizza and a little bit of money. With the disrobing thoughts still in the back of my mind, I headed south again to Houston. I got about a mile again when the thought came up that I should go back to Popeyes, get naked, and show them my driver's license and social security card. I pushed those thoughts down a little but still got rid of the church offerings in another city drain. I made it another fifty yards when the thought came up that I should go back to Popeyes again. This time, I got rid of everything but the clothes I was wearing.

I went about a mile along Highway I-45 and stopped in a Starbucks to ask for water. They gave me ice water, and then I was on my journey to Houston. I wasn't sure if I could go to the Salvation Army without credentials because of a past experience there, but I wanted to get to Houston and escape the Popeyes disrobing thoughts. As I was walking along the highway, I saw another Popeyes Chicken up ahead. I decided to venture back into a neighborhood to try and avoid this Popeyes. I was getting very thirsty and was constantly challenged to stay on the sidewalk and not even barely touch any property that was not private unless I had a valid legal reason to be on their property.

I eventually threw my empty water cup in someone's ditch and felt like I needed to apologize, so I knocked on their door to tell them I was sorry. A young man answered and indicated that it was okay. While I was there, I asked him for some water, and he gave me bottled water. I witnessed to him about God, and his dad came home and got suspicious, so I left. I eventually asked another man for help with bus fare, and he gave me some change. After doing this several times, I eventually made it into Houston and stayed the night on a bench in Heights Park.

The bench was hard, and the mosquitos were relentless. The birds also kept chirping throughout the night. I woke up to the sound of joggers making noise as their feet crushed the gravelly dirt below them. What was I to do now? I felt horrible about getting rid of all my IDs, awards, and personal information. What would happen if I died? My poor parents wouldn't know about it. How would I start a new life in Houston with absolutely nothing but the clothes on my back?

I began to venture the trails in the Heights and beyond into the Houston area. I came across a bum and asked him where I might get food and if he knew of anyone that could help me get new IDs. He told me about several charities in the area. I went to one of the charities, and they gave me lunch and told me to come back on a certain day to work on getting new IDs. Apparently, they worked with a number of agencies to help get you official papers needed to get a new birth certificate and other identifying information.

Each night, the mosquitos would have a heyday on my body. After a few days of boredom walking around the Heights and Houston, I thought I should go back to street preaching. One of the benches I slept at had a World War II memorial nearby, and across the street was a booming coffee shop with outdoor patrons. In order to know where to preach, I would go to different locations and then pray if it was God's will. If I didn't feel moved or didn't feel right after belting out a few scriptures, then I would move on to another location. Here I was in the same clothes for days on end, preaching on random corners along Heights Boulevard. I was getting tired of living on the benches in the Heights. One night, I decided I would try to venture forty miles to La Marque, Texas, where my church was. I didn't make it very far through the west side of Houston before crashing in another park on a park bench for the night.

The next day, as I was walking around west Houston, I felt the urge to preach, so I picked a random street corner and prayed about it there. I ended up backing out of the preaching and decided to walk away from that area and now tried to avoid the street-preaching thoughts. I would walk around the city of Houston nonstop. My body was down to about 130 pounds. I wasn't looking good. I would get exhausted walking and just sit down on sidewalks in random places. Eventually, I made it back to the Heights benches where I previously stayed.

As I was walking around that area, my OCD about stepping on people's property flared up. I would feel like I needed to apologize, give them any change in my pocket, and get naked to prostrate myself before them in guilt and reconciliation. I was running from one place to another to try and get rid of the naked thoughts and get far away from the houses where I stepped on property. After a number of days of wearing the same thing and walking the Heights trail, this paranoid woman came up to me and threatened to call the police if I didn't leave the area.

I hastily decided to leave the area. As I was walking down a street, I decided to get rid of my pants and long-sleeved shirt, but I had khaki shorts and short-sleeved shirt underneath. But this was one step closer to disrobing. Something was working on my mind. I was constantly on the run. I eventually ran into the highway heading into downtown Houston. I decided to walk the shoulder of the highway and head as far south as I could. As I was walking on a long elevated highway, this couple, a Black man and White girl, offered to drive me down the road. I witnessed to them about God and told the Black guy I wanted to go as far south as possible. He dropped me off at the University of Houston, and they gave me five dollars.

I ended up walking all around midtown and part of downtown Houston and over near the University of Houston. I was trying to find a place to rest my head and eventually settled for a tall grassy patch in between the highway and feeder road. It seemed like a safe bet, since any other place would be in a bad neighborhood nearby, and I was embedded in the tall grass in the dark of night.

Morning came, and I decided once again to try and venture down the highway toward La Marque, Texas, about thirty-five miles south where I could go to my church. I needed help spiritually, I thought, not realizing mentally I wasn't in the right place in life.

As I walked along the feeder road near the University of Houston, a homeless man with a cup for collecting contributions asked me if I could give him some money. I had no money, but the silly thought crossed my mind to give him my shirt. I fought the thought because I didn't want to be walking around

Houston with just shorts and shoes on. I quickly walked away from the area and, after about an hour, ended up at a park with other homeless individuals. I was plagued by the thought of the shirt. I asked a homeless guy if he knew of any ministries around that I could get a shirt from. I thought that I would then be able to go back and give my shirt to that other homeless guy with a collections cup and have one for me.

While waiting at the homeless park, I was plagued by "giving away my shirt" thoughts, so I decided I would head back to that area from the morning where the homeless guy with the cup was. As I was walking through a neighborhood, I saw a building storage area with a bunch of bananas. I asked the guy standing by the bananas if I could have some because I was very hungry. He said they were not safe, and as I began walking away, he called me back and gave me a bunch of snack food. I walked down the road and felt like the food wasn't from God, so I left it on a bench at a bus stop. I eventually made my way back to the place of the homeless guy with the cup, but he wasn't there.

Another homeless guy came up to me and mockingly offered to give me a hug. I was uncomfortable in the area, so I ventured north back toward downtown Houston. I felt estranged from God and plagued with condemning thoughts for not giving away my shirt. As I walked down the road, I saw a little piece of paper on the ground that said "Jesus loves you" from a charismatic Catholic church. Maybe a sign? It didn't hold in my mind, and I walked toward downtown. I eventually made it to another park in the city and took a nap behind a water fountain on a bench.

I stayed downtown till evening and then got an idea to try and panhandle enough change to get on a bus and perhaps head north to my parents' house in Spring, thirty miles away. I was getting desperate to have a change of scene and get away from thoughts of giving away my shirt, which was leading down a slippery slope of eventually becoming naked, which we'll address later.

As night rolled in, I was able to get a couple of bucks from a stranger, and he looked up a bus on his smartphone that would get me further north, towards my parents' home. I finally got on a bus, and my mind was clouded with thoughts telling me not to go to Spring. I was in an internal war, trying to reason my way out of a deluded spiritual understanding that I was to stay in my directionless existence in Houston and continue with weird spiritual tirades. That night, I made it to an area called Greenspoint, also known to some as Guns Point for its reputation for crime. I spent the night on a bench at a bus stop. In the night, a young man on a bicycle stopped to talk to me. He was very talkative and probably figured I was just another bum to pour out his thoughts to while I was trying to sleep.

Morning came, and I got on another bus that got me to a road called Farm to Market 1960, 12 miles from Spring. I was walking down a road called

Kuykendahl. As I was walking this road with no shoulder on the side, I was doing everything possible not to touch the adjacent grass because I knew my mind would tell me I had to apologize to landowners along this road for being on their property. I made it to a little side road and sat down on the road. I was weak and tired of fighting this property concern.

A man in an adjacent parking lot saw me sitting there in the road and said I needed help. I told him I was trying to walk to my parents' house in Spring. He told me that I should call the police and ask them for a ride. While my intuition told me that's not what the police are for, I was tired, so I gave in to the man's suggestion. I called the police from a nearby store's phone that they graciously offered. The police came and questioned me and told me that I should call my parents for the ride. I called my parents and told them that I had parted ways with all my identification, that I was living on the streets, and asked if they could come get me and let me live at their place. Being good parents like they are, they came within the hour.

6

OCD Led Me to the Tracks

My mother and father drove me to a McDonald's to buy me food, and then they drove me to the original location of my truck that I had previously abandoned. We got my truck back to their house, and I stayed there for about a day. I kept feeling like I needed to go back to the Heights to preach on street corners. My parents were afraid for me and stayed up late to try and talk me into staying with them. I have forgiven myself to this day but sometimes feel bad for what I put them through, though I know I had a mental illness that was causing all this, so I don't blame myself. To this day, my parents are loving and understanding.

In the middle of the night, I got up and walked a couple of miles south. I stayed the night in a grassy area between the highway and feeder road. While I could hear the traffic, it was the only place where most people don't suspect a homeless person sleeping in the night.

As weird as it is to be sleeping in grass by a highway, for some reason, I felt very peaceful. I have later come to discover that peace is good, but our brains are also wired in a normal person to be on alert and not accept this kind of lifestyle. Something in me should not have been at peace with this. Maslow's hierarchy of needs tells us that we should be unsettled with settling for the beggarly elements of life. God wired in us a sense of survival and thriving, and I was not considering either scenario at this stage of my life. My hyperreligious delusions had set me on a course of purely cause and effect of my mind and not constructive thinking about what is overall good and healthy in life. This would come later with understanding God's great love and grace for each of us.

As the sun came up, I got up out of the grass and brushed the debris off me from the night's sleep. I was getting thinner, my sneakers were wearing out, and my shorts and shirt were very loose on my bony body. I walked further south and went to a street corner near an AutoZone Auto Parts store. I was thinking about preaching there. I was struggling with thoughts of doing something unconventional like doing a headstand on the street corner to get people's attention and maybe use it as a witnessing tool. I was starting to believe God wanted me to do this.

I fought this and started to walk away from the street corner. As I was walking along the side of the road, a friendly man in about his forties pulled by in a truck and asked me if I needed anything. I asked for something to eat, and he ended up giving me a $20 bill. I also asked if he knew of any good churches, though I had already been thinking about a particular church near the AutoZone I was at. He drove me a few miles up the road and dropped me off at a Baptist church he said that he had been to before and liked, though he didn't stay, and we parted ways.

After getting a bite at a convenience store, I walked two miles back to that other church near the AutoZone. I went in there in casual shorts, T-shirt, and tennis shoes, slightly dirty from sleeping the night before in the grass, and after service, went to the front of the altar for prayer. As funny as this sounds, the woman praying over me said something along the lines of, "God doesn't need you to do a headstand," without me telling her of the headstand concern.

After service, I asked some of the staff if they knew of any charities I might visit to get food. One minister gave me a $20 bill. I first took it and then tried to give it back, but he insisted I take it. We talked for a little while, and I told him how I had thrown all my IDs down the drain in Houston, and he said that is a sign I am "certifiable," a.k.a. "mental."

After our talk, I walked about a quarter mile to a McDonald's and had some McChicken sandwiches. I was then thinking I might go back to my parents but couldn't decide. I walked a little in the direction back toward their house through a neighborhood and ended up stopping at a garage sale. The lady running a garage sale had bid on a whole estate and was selling it in front of her house. We began to talk a lot. I talked about one day maybe becoming a pastor, and she took a liking to me. She made me a number of sandwiches, and as the day rolled into night, she insisted she take me back to my parents' house. So that night, I knocked on their door, and my dad opened it and let me stay, of course.

That night, I told my dad about going to a church and meeting the lady from the garage sale. He seemed happy that I was back.

The next morning, I noticed my parents had cleaned my truck out and did laundry with all my clothes and blankets stored in there from my prior months living at the Walmart. Later that day, at my dad's insistence, I agreed I would go see a counselor in the coming days that he made an appointment with. As I was at the house, I was struggling with feeling peace about being there. I kept thinking that God wanted me to move on. I also, as part of my delusional state, didn't think I needed to see a counselor and ended up backing out of it, to my father's disappointment.

My niece from out of state called me and tried to talk me into staying at my parents' home. She offered to send one of her older friends over to take me to movies, to get out, and get my mind in a better place, but I passed up the offer, being restless about being at my parents' home. As another day passed, the unpeaceful restless feelings, including thinking God wanted me to move on, were overwhelming, and I ended up leaving my parents' house again.

I walked a couple of miles back to the AutoZone street corner location and was standing there thinking about preaching. This gentleman named Robert, about my age and much healthier looking, came up to me and asked me if he could pray for me. He had been looking for ways to reach out to people with his faith, and I guess I was an easy target. I was delighted to have the intervention, and we prayed together. He then took me to a Wendy's burger joint, and we ate and talked about Bible scriptures.

Later, he took me to his aunt's house. We talked throughout the night, and she let me go into her refrigerator and make whatever I wanted. I ate and ate and ate, and she encouraged it. I thought the solution to my constant going from place to place with preaching and other hyperreligious thoughts would be solved if I got back to my church in La Marque, Texas. So the next morning, Robert agreed to drive me down there, sixty-five miles away. On the way, Robert and I did a tag-team ministry outreach where he would go up to street people at this gas station and witness to them about God while I prayed over him for safety and effectiveness. Then he would take a break and pray for me while I preached on a street corner across from the gas station by the highway. I didn't preach very long before feeling like we should call it quits and get back on our way to La Marque.

As we drove down the highway, we would quote scriptures and talk about my new life to be in La Marque. Maybe a family from the church would let me stay with them. Robert had known my pastor there from a prior church conference where my pastor had visited his church. I arrived in the church lobby, very scrawny, and asked the pastor's daughter if she knew of anyone I might be able to stay with until I got back on my feet. She arranged for me to talk with a church leader. We talked for about an hour, and he recommended I go back to my parents sixty-five miles north.

I was very torn and felt like I should just stay in the area and live as a street person so I could attend my church. I told Robert and decided to go back to my parents, all the while battling in my mind about not having peace with this. I was in an internal struggle. I had been running from place to place, getting thin, living on whatever food I could get from kind souls, freshening up in random store bathrooms, struggling with hyperreligious thoughts about preaching, thinking I was trespassing by barely touching others' property, etc.

We got back to my parents' house, and my mother was so delighted that the church sent me back. However, she would still face more disappointment after I ate half a sandwich and told her I would be on my way again. I left on a Sunday around 6:00 p.m. I began to walk the feeder road of the highway, but this time, going north toward Conroe, Texas. I was thinking about maybe walking ten miles to Conroe and trying to stay at the Salvation Army there. Sometimes I would veer back into an adjacent neighborhood by the highway because I was concerned my parents might try to track me down, and I wanted to be incognito. I happened to have a new copy of my birth certificate and temporary driver's license my parents helped me get during my short stay with them after they rescued me a few weeks back.

The OCD or hyperreligiosity was getting strong again, and as I was resting by a light pole on the side of highway, I set my birth certificate and temporary ID by the pole, which was only to be temporary in my mind while I rested. However, I then felt like I had littered by resting my paperwork there and that the paperwork was no longer mine but the state's because I had set it on their highway right-of-way. I tried to fight this and picked up my documents and continued my way down the highway, but the thought just wouldn't go away. Hours went by with the struggle, and I was getting tired of thinking about it, so I eventually set it down by another light pole at an intersection near a community college. I still had more IDs coming in the mail (Social Security card and permanent driver's license) that I figured would be in safekeeping when they arrived at my parents' address, though I didn't know if or when I would be back there, as I always had a struggle staying there.

I stayed the night in a grassy median of Highway 242 near the Woodlands, Texas, and the next morning, rested under a bridge near a creek. I noticed a few deer grazing. I then walked the hike and bike trails of the Woodlands, Texas, and found myself at a park with a pond. I spent the day as usual, thinking about my condition and meditating on spiritual matters. I got up and began walking the hike and bike trails with plans to eventually get back to the main highway. I had abandoned the prior plan to go to the Salvation Army in Conroe, Texas, as it was quite a walk, and I was getting more and more worn down.

As I was making my way through the Woodlands trails, I would stop by parks to rest. At one park, disrobing thoughts entered my head, and I kept thinking maybe God wanted me to disrobe. The other part of me pushed back, but I was fighting these hyper-religious urges, so I walked as fast as I could from that park and confessed scripture to try and get the thoughts out of my head. My new goal was to get out of the Woodlands, so I walked at a very brisk pace for miles on end in this fight. That night, I finally made it to a bridge overpass at the main highway in Spring, Texas, and slept under the bridge.

The next morning, I woke up and took a restroom break behind the plants, hidden from traffic near the bridge. I began to walk west and didn't make it very far before having intrusive thoughts about being naked. I was frustrated, so I cried out to God with my hands raised high to the sky. A man from the Salvation Army selling newspapers saw me and came over to comfort me. He gave me a $5 gift certificate to a Jack in the Box on the other side of the highway near the bridge and told me to not worry, that everything would be okay. I walked into the Jack in the Box and got a coffee and a breakfast sandwich. About the time I was eating, my parents walked into the restaurant. They had contacted the man who had helped me before, Robert, the street minister, and he tipped them off that I may be in that area near the highway, which wasn't far from the AutoZone I previously met him at.

My parents wanted to take me to a doctor for a physical checkup as I was down to 130 pounds, and they were concerned. They also wanted to make me breakfast at home. They were hoping the doctor might see my overall condition and recommend mental help, but he simply asked a number of questions and released me. I didn't realize the mental help was their motive at the time. After talking to them later in life, they couldn't believe that the doctor didn't probe more as to my gaunt condition. We had breakfast at their house after that, which eggs and fried Spam tacos. Sounds kind of gross to some, but to me, was a treasured meal. The evening rolled around, and once again, as usual, I felt like

God wanted me to move on, which I know today was my religious delusion.

After leaving my folks in the evening, I walked about a mile north in the neighborhood, then a mile east, and then a mile back south along a road adjacent to railroad tracks. I was having the issues with being concerned about walking on other people's property, even if just barely next to the road. I ended up stepping on a little business property and was frustrated. I knew I was going to have to clear this concern in my head. I didn't want to apologize to them. So I decided to stand near the railroad tracks across from their business and pray about the situation. I was thinking of maybe waiting till the business closed and there would be no one to apologize to. Then I was planning to walk the railroad tracks twenty-six miles to Houston when evening broke. I was standing in the same spot for hours praying, lifting my hands to God, and biding my time.

The neighborhood residents that saw me began to get worried and made a number of calls to the police department. As I was standing there, I was tired, hungry, and sick of sleeping in random places outside. I prayed to God: "God, I would like something to eat and a comfortable bed to rest in tonight."

Not long after that prayer, a cop pulled up who knew me from walking my parents' neighborhood in the past. He said, "Thomas, I can't make you do this, but I would like for you to go to the hospital for a general checkup." To be honest, I wasn't sure if that was God's will in my mind, and I knew we shouldn't use the hospital system but decided it would be a nice night of food and good rest in a comfortable hospital bed and decided to do it with perhaps the wrong motives for going to a hospital.

7

The Mental Ward

The hospital stay was interesting. The doctor asked me a few questions, and I spewed off a bunch of religious talk and how I got from place to place, praying to escape the last situation I found myself in. Even at this point, I had not come to any conclusions that I had a mental problem. To me, everything was a spiritual battle that I believed, as a Christian, had some truth, but I wasn't able to have insight that I needed help on this earth from people. Today, I know I was sick mentally at that time. Though it doesn't negate parts of that process where I had genuine faith, I was just dealing with a mixture of true faith at some points and hyperreligiosity that was not healthy or right.

Later that night, in my hospital bed, they set me up on a videoconference with a mental health professional. I told her how I would walk all over the Woodlands with bad thoughts (I didn't want to tell her what) and try to escape by walking fast and quoting scripture. "Like I was the apostle Paul on a secret mission," I said to her. Though that is silly as the apostle Paul was a mighty man of God that did real exploits within the true Christian faith.

Lying in bed, I was worried about the "getting naked in public" thoughts and thought I might share with someone, but I didn't fully convey this. I only told one of the nurses that I had very strange thoughts and felt I needed help. She encouraged me with kind words. A little later, I wrote those thoughts on a piece of paper and held on to it.

As a new nurse came in the next day and began to talk to me, I ripped the paper up in little pieces in front of her. She asked, "What was that?"

I said, "Nothing. It's something that was bothering me, but God is helping me."

She kind of smiled and said, "Thomas, Thomas," like she knew I needed help.

The whole next day, I constantly talked to the nurse about the Bible. It was full-on witnessing and preaching. I still believe in God's Word, but that day might have been much for her, and we have to be sensitive to the Holy Spirit and not cram down what we believe on others but let God get in our words in love; though the Bible does say, "Always be ready to give an account of the hope that is in you."

As the day was coming to a close, another head nurse told me she wanted me to voluntarily be escorted and agree to check into a mental health hospital they had coordinated with. She said if I didn't volunteer to do it that she would have a "mental health warrant" be put out on me, and eventually, the police would take me there. I refused at first, and she seemed not happy about it.

Later, the ambulance showed up, and for some reason, a young nurse lady from the ambulance talked me into it. She said it would be better to go voluntarily and then you could get released easier as being involuntarily admitted might create more problems. On our ride to the mental hospital, I was witnessing to the young nurse lady. She asked me if I came from a cult. She said, "Everything you talk is Bible talk, and I have never heard anybody like that." I, of course, brushed it off, thinking she was attacking my faith. But I was not too concerned. On the way to the mental hospital, I decided I didn't want to go, so I told the nurse. She called her supervisor, and he said that they had to take me there and couldn't let me out of the ambulance.

I arrived behind locked doors in a sitting area with a few other patients. While I was there, I was convinced this was all baloney and that I didn't have a problem. I decided not to sign the voluntary papers. I felt peace about it, but that peace was more, I believe, just God allowing me to do what I felt comfortable with in that situation. In life, though, I was going to need a little help; eventually, that happened.

Hours later, after a judge ordered my admittance, they moved me into the main mental health ward. It was late at night, and the other patients were asleep in their rooms. After being frisked in a small padded room and given flip-flop sandals (as they don't want you to have shoes with shoelaces to prevent potential suicides of patients), they took me out of the room and offered me something to eat. A big Black friendly man offered to make me peanut butter and jelly sandwiches, as the kitchen at that hour was closed. They were delicious. I scarfed those babies down, and then they showed me to my room for the night.

The next morning, around 7:00 a.m., they woke us all up, and it was breakfast time. The food came in these big plastic trays. Everything was plastic, and they watched us eat. In these places, everything is geared around not letting a patient hurt themselves or others. I scarfed down my hot breakfast, and then they had this volunteer come in and play like a DJ, and we could request songs. The first song I remember them playing was "Happy" by Pharrell Williams. I could tell by some of the faces of others that they felt estranged and not really happy. It was dawning on me that there really are folks needing mental help, as I was never really a part of this world.

After DJ hour, I was in my room, praying, and a psychiatrist showed up. He asked me what brought me to the institution. I went over my story of being at the railroad tracks a few days back for a number of hours praying, and how people were concerned about me. He put me on Risperdal that is used for multiple mental disorders. I refused to take it at first. That night, after a meal, I suspected the medicine had been added to my food, as afterward I was feeling a slight lightheadedness and drowsiness. Eventually, I complied with taking the medicine because the medicine lady told me I could get out quicker that way, if I went with the program.

Each day, I would stand in the back of the room about twenty-five feet from the TV that some were sitting around. I would pray and quote scripture. I began to have problems at mealtimes. I would have intrusive curse word thoughts toward God and wouldn't feel right eating a meal right after that, so I began to skip meals. About thirty minutes before each meal, I would pray and try to focus on good things and keep the curse-word thoughts from coming. Little distractions from others in the institution would set the thoughts off. It was like walking a tightrope, because I didn't want to miss meals.

One day, this girl saw me in line for dinner as I was struggling, and she knew it and began to laugh hysterically at me. I don't judge her because she had her own issues. Sometimes people would notice me not eating and say, "You're going to get sick if you don't eat." I didn't share with them my dilemma with the curse-word thoughts. I may get into this phenomenon later but will say that no matter what's on your mind, God wants you to eat. The thoughts may have been mine or not, but I realize his grace now and unconditional love.

One day in the institution, while walking around with a Bible that they gave me at my request, a girl of Puerto Rican descent came up to me and asked me if I was reading a novel. I said, "Well, I'm reading the Bible."

She was curious and would ask me questions about it. I gave a short synopsis of man's fall and rebellion, our inherited sinful state, and what God did with his Son Jesus out of love to redeem us. I asked her if she would like to pray a prayer and have 100 percent assurance of a new life and salvation. She said yes, and we prayed the sinner's prayer based on the book of Romans, chapter 10, verses 9 through 13, in Jesus's name.

After concluding the prayer, I felt a peaceful presence, and she looked at me as if she just felt something too. We began to be friends, and I found out she was struggling with an identity issue. She would ask me if she was a girl. I know nowadays what I'm going to say may get me in trouble with the "woke police," but I kindly affirmed to her that she was a girl, and every time I said that, she seemed relieved and happy and wanted to get to know me more.

We would go to the church services they had on Sundays downstairs that they escorted us to from the main mental ward. At some point, she wanted a romantic relationship, but I didn't think this is what the Lord wanted. I gave her some brotherly advice to begin reading the Bible, and when she got out of the place to find a good Bible-believing, Spirit-filled church with her newfound faith. I also advised her to surround herself with other female believers to encourage her in her faith.

A few days later, I saw her reading a black Bible. I believed I might have been more helpful, but I was still going through lots of issues (what I thought were just spiritual, not mental), including missing meals and feeling my peace disturbed by others with issues in the place.

After a couple of weeks in the institution, a team of psychologists had a question-and-answer session with me. I told them about all the wandering around from place to place and preaching on street corners and not wanting to walk on private property. At this point, I still wouldn't admit to myself that my issues merited mental help from professionals as I thought they were just spiritual warfare, so I was trying to mind my p's and q's other than struggling with meals to get out of the ward.

I eventually got transferred to a program in the neighboring ward that would help me get housing, a job, and back on my feet. It was a pilot program in the state of Texas with special funding. However, I continued to think these kinds of things weren't God's will for me and, ultimately, did not go along with it and requested out.

When I took a special written exam requested by them to get more insight into my issues, I answered the questions very cleverly so as to never get into the past castration thoughts and disrobing thoughts. Looking back, I should have just spilled the beans. After over a month in the institution, they discharged me. I didn't want to go back to my parents, as I knew in times past that I wouldn't have peace there—not by their fault; I was just misguided in my beliefs that God didn't want me there. So I ended up at the Star of Hope in Houston the evening of my discharge.

That evening, at the Star of Hope, I called a lady by the name of Margaret who was the aunt of Robert, the man who ministered to me about six weeks earlier back near my parents' home. She had mental issues in her past and had been previously calling me at the mental institution to try and convince me I should be there. She found out I got discharged in our phone call, and she was alarmed. She thought I may have Asperger syndrome and that I should have stayed in that pilot program. She told me I wasn't ready to be out of the institution and I should try and figure out a way to get back in.

At this point in my life, I was kind of agreeing that I had problems but not fully bought in. However, I believed her in this conversation, so I told the people at the Star of Hope I was not feeling mentally stable, in hopes that I would somehow end up back in the institution. Though part of myself previously in the institution was full-on in what I thought God's will was, which was to stay out of the mental health world, another part of me was slowly buying that there was a problem, and perhaps professional help was a good thing. It would come a little later in my life where I fully bought into the mental illness, and it wasn't long after that point that I made tremendous progress, which we will get to.

So that evening, at the Star of Hope, a police officer showed up. By the word *unstable* I used earlier in describing my state, they probably thought it was something sinister or dangerous. He actually cuffed me and drove me to another mental health hospital. After all I had been through, I didn't care about the cuffs, though the nurse at the hospital rightfully looked disgusted by the officer's behavior.

That night, a psychiatrist asked a battery of questions, and I decided to tell him about the religious castration thoughts that started a year and a half ago, though they weren't bothering me at that time. Ultimately, after he looked over my prior mental institution admittance and discharge, he decided I just needed to stay on medicine and go live with family. He also diagnosed me with schizophrenia. My dad came and picked me up that night.

8

To Disrobe or Not to Disrobe?

M y time with my parents was short-lived as I insisted to them they take me to the Star of Hope shelter in Houston. As usual, I had the misconception and lack of peace to stay there. Though I realize now that sometimes we just have to push through feelings, and God typically doesn't guide us by feelings. Actually, what happened was that I left their place while they were taking my sister to the airport, and on their way back, they saw me walking, and I told them my plan to go to Houston. They realized I was going to do what I wanted, which was totally misguided in my mind, and they decided to be supportive and drive me to the Star of Hope.

I arrived at the Star of Hope in the late afternoon and got this feeling in my mind that I could be free and go anywhere. Perhaps I would walk or hitchhike back to my original church in La Marque, Texas. I bought a few tacos at a taco truck stand with a little cash my dad gave me. I was starting to have the thought that I wasn't supposed to receive help from my parents, that it wasn't God's will, so I took my wallet that had new IDs they helped me get and threw them in a trash can.

As I was walking in the area near Buffalo Bayou later, I saw a Black man totally disrobe in front of me. Can you say trigger? I pushed it out of my mind at that time and got out of that area quickly. Later that night, I ended up at the Salvation Army a couple miles away.

The next morning, one of the men at the shelter told me about this place where I could relax and drink all the coffee I wanted. I followed him there. On the way there, I was having second thoughts about the wallet I threw away. I checked back at that trash can, but it had been emptied.

After roaming the streets for a few days, I ended up at a park and ran into a man that claimed to be an apostle. He called himself Apostle Mark. He was homeless and preached to me his take on the doctrine of sin and how that plays out in a believer's life. He was preaching that the believer cannot sin and had an interesting way of expressing this. While the Bible says a believer does not habitually sin, sin is reality that happens, but the believer is covered and made righteous by Jesus's sacrifice. I will spare discussion on this topic right now. Needless to say, I was still intrigued by his explanations. I began to get comfortable with him and unloaded some things that bothered me in life. I figured, *Why not?* This is a random guy, and this might be a good opportunity. I told him that I thought God wanted me to disrobe in public. He immediately insisted that was not right, but for some reason, after I told him this, the thoughts began to get really strong.

From then on, for about two days, I battled all day long the thought of disrobing, though I didn't want to do it, but I wanted to please God in my twisted view of things at that time. I was getting so frustrated that I actually told a random police officer, and he talked me down, saying that would not be good if a child saw it. Still, it wouldn't go away. At some point, I thought about waiting till I saw a police officer again and then just doing it right there in front of him so I could get quickly arrested and not too many people would see me. Perhaps it was OCD or psychosis or a combination of both, but the urges were getting stronger and stronger. At one point, while not actively thinking about killing myself, I had some suicidal ideations that it might be nice.

Eventually, I made my way to another police station, went in, and told the administrative lady I was having bad thoughts and needed help. I told the lady, "God is telling me to get naked in public." I told her that I got out of a mental institution six days prior and desperately needed to be back there. I was grappling and rebelling in my mind to the perceived God's will to disrobe in public and wanted to get myself out of the public as soon as possible to not do it. I was disobeying this perceived command. I got escorted in a cop car to a mental hospital.

Not long at the first mental hospital which was only for a few nights stay, they transferred me back to the one I had been at originally (Harris County Psychiatric Center). My time this second round was darker and seemed totally different from the first time. Every day, the doctor would ask me if the thoughts were any better after giving me medicine, but everything they did was to no avail. I still thought God wanted me to get naked but now in the institution, since that's where I was confined to. I fought it every day and eventually got transferred to another unit. I was seeing all the same doctors as before.

After these thoughts persisted for days on end, I succumbed to the urges. I was standing in a particular spot, trying to time it out where I would disrobe and then run into a bathroom in a way that males could see me but not females as my religious side said that would be okay but not good for the women. I stripped down and quickly paced about thirty feet to a bathroom. A male nurse and several men saw it. The male nurse got on me, saying, "You can't do that in here."

I asked him to bring my clothes to the restroom so I could put them back on. While I was in this second ward unit; once again, they had intended to put me back in that long-term pilot program for housing, work, etc., but the actual disrobing incident disqualified me from this.

After complying with their requests and no longer disrobing in the mental institution, they eventually discharged me. From this point on, I would bounce around between various county housing units in a special program called Critical Time Intervention that I applied for about a month after my stay at Harris County Psychiatric Center. I would be in various programs designed to get in group therapy interactions. All the while at these places, I still pursued the street preaching. At one point, I did not fully comply with my caseworker's instructions to apply to a state program called Department of Assistive and Rehabilitation Services, which would have extended my housing needs. I kept having strong feelings telling me to rely on God and not these programs. I look back on it and realize there would have been nothing wrong to get the help. But, I couldn't distinguish between strong opposing feelings that I thought were God versus God's real will. I know today his will would have been to get all the help I could. I ended up back at the Star of Hope homeless shelter.

While at the Star of Hope, an older Black man who reminded me of Morgan Freeman, showed me all the freebies in downtown Houston. We went to several day shelters for food, laundry services, and social services we could apply to. We walked the underground tunnels of Houston. We went to the library, where he showed me how he would read certain books while there and put his bookmarks in them for the next time he came back. At the Star of Hope, he preferred sleeping on a hard mat instead of the beds there. He had once been an editor for a magazine. He seemed to have come to a place of accepting his current reality as a Star of Hope resident that wandered the streets of Houston every day.

At the Star of Hope, there were many people with mental issues. I eventually got overwhelmed with a certain resident who wanted to be buddy-buddy and always hang around me and try to persuade me of certain doctrines in the Bible I disagreed with. He was kind of overbearing, and I really just wanted to be away from him. Eventually, I left the Star of Hope, as this person was disturbing my peace every time I was there. Being back on the streets was not good for me. And once again, the disrobing thoughts in public started rearing their ugly head. Days later, after the urges were very strong again, I ended up back at Harris County Psychiatric Center.

At the mental ward, it wasn't but a day or two, and I decided to disrobe, thinking this was God's will. I disrobed near my bedroom and walked up to the front counter. They saw me, and then I walked back to my room to put my clothes back on. Every day, the thought would come up, but I fought it throughout the rest of my stay there. I shared it with a friend there, and he would try to talk me down on it. Many times, I requested antianxiety medicine to try and buffer the thoughts. After a month there, and with good behavior, they released me once again.

9

A Blueprint of Recovery
from Jesus

After a weeklong stay at the YMCA paid for by
my parents, for the first time in a long time,
I would finally return to their place. With sugges-
tions from a number of people, I applied for Social
Security Disability. I discussed on the application

how I believed sometimes God wanted me to disrobe in public. They also had access to my number of stays at the mental health hospital and all the doctor's records. Within a very short period, I was approved for Social Security Disability. However, the hyperreligious side of me kept thinking this is not what God wanted and that I should give the money back to Social Security and request my benefits be cancelled.

In order to cancel your benefits, you had to fill out a form, get two witnesses, and send all the money back. For about three months, I didn't touch the money. I was split on whether I should send it all back or not. I rebelled against my perception of God's will and went out and bought a Jeep. That way, I would lock myself in and not be able to repay them or, in other words, keep myself from cancelling the benefits.

About six months after being at my parents' house, I decided to pray to God again about the disrobing thoughts. I believed for the first time I was hearing him right, and he was saying to let that go. The castration thoughts are also something that came up twice again in my future, and God gave me assurance that was not his will. He helped me to see that for what it is, something completely outside his will to do such self-harm and in a humiliating way. For about two years after the last time at the mental institution, life was getting better.

I had one final area that was resurfacing, and that was the thought that God was telling me to move to Galveston and do miming gestures on the seawall, something I had done about six years prior. The obsession with Galveston lasted about six months, including numerous trips there, a stay twice at a rooming house, multiple motel stays, several stays at the Salvation Army, and some short-lived attempts at doing the gestures in dressy clothes on the seawall. Things didn't seem the same as they had six years ago, and the gestures didn't seem like an effective tool for bringing the gospel to people as opposed to one-on-one conversations and supporting the local church who supports missions.

After the OCD obsessions with doing religious gestures ceased, with new medication and journaling, I began to have hope again for my future. Life was starting to look up. I had this feeling that I would be in a better place, that God still had something up his sleeve for me, but this time, not in a weird hyperreligious way.

During my journaling period, I would also listen to sermons by a grace preacher from Singapore. I slowly began to realize how secure I was in God's love for me, and nothing could separate that because of my faith in Jesus who sacrificed himself to save me from myself. I started working for a relative in a construction business, dating, volunteering, and going on job interviews. I took up the hobby of singing karaoke on smartphone apps, Smule and StarMaker, and it became a very enriching pastime. To date, I love to sing.

Today, I work in the engineering industry. I have a stable job, my own place, and great relationships with family and friends. I am healed of hyper-religiosity. For those of you that believe in Jesus or want to know more, God has healed me by helping me think differently about his love and covenant of grace, which is unearned, undeserved, unmerited favor. He has shown me the finality of what Jesus did on the cross once for all eternity as it says in the book of Hebrews. Jesus is at rest, sitting at God's right hand as the work of the cross is finished, and all sins (past, present, and future) can now be imputed to the work of Jesus at the cross.

Once you know you are God's child by faith in Jesus, you can have full assurance that he will never abandon you and that your salvation is permanent. One factor that did not help me during the prior hyperreligious mental illness was thinking I had to walk a very tight rope and that I could lose my salvation. I am a walking witness of what that kind of thinking taken to the extreme can do. I am free today. I still have occasional weird thoughts about God, but I'm able to quickly diffuse that based on all I have been through, the breakthroughs I made in journaling, and listening to grace messages about Jesus.

The Bible says in 2 Corinthians 5:21 that Jesus, who never sinned, took on all sin on himself at the cross so that he could impart right standing to you with the Father. Jesus gifts us his righteousness in place of our self-righteousness, which falls short of the glory of God. It's a divine exchange. That gift means that when you make a mistake, if you are a believer in Jesus, all God sees is his perfect Son in you. You are blameless because of the blood of Jesus shed for you.

This book was written to share my journey and let all know there is hope for you, no matter what situation you have found yourself in life. You have not gone too far to turn things around for the better. Several important things I hold dear and have learned also in my healing process and maintaining good health are as follows:

- Never hold things in. If you are experiencing any kind of distressing thoughts, find a trusted person you can talk to. Also, depending on the severity of the thoughts, there is no shame in seeking professional help. Looking back at my life, I would have sought professional help early on around the time I thought God wanted me to prophesy on a desk to my work, like John the Baptist.

- Always maintain healthy boundaries in your life. We can burn out through over-commitment, people-pleasing, negative people in our lives, pushing ourselves too hard, and setting unreasonable expectations for ourselves. Don't be afraid to say no, and do what is good for you. This is not selfish. If you aren't at your best in life, then your help to others is not at its best. Help yourself first. Then from that, you can help and love others.

- Practice unconditional self-love. Give yourself room to make mistakes. Pursue excellence but not perfection. Excellence allows you to do what you can within reason, without regard for faults, and go forward. Perfectionism leads to self-condemnation and negative thoughts when you don't measure up. God wants you to walk in grace, his favor on you, because of his love for you in which he doesn't keep a tally of your mistakes.

- Be honest with yourself. Another major pivot point in my healing above is when I began to journal and look at my life from the outside in. When I began to realize that my life and many of the things I did were unhealthy and didn't make sense, I owned up to the fact that I had a mental condition. Owning the reality of my condition allowed me to begin healing and also know that God knows my condition and is not being hard on me.

- Ask God to give you grace to forgive others in your life. Forgiveness is for you. When you forgive others, it releases you to go on in life. I have come to learn that you can forgive others by faith, even if you don't feel it. I do it by praying to God, saying, "Father, I forgive and release that person by faith," and then I pray for good things for them. This goes contrary to our human nature, but it is very liberating. I have kept good relationships by not letting offense push me away. When you realize that you have faults, and God put them on Jesus at the cross, it becomes easier to let others' faults go. If that person is unsafe to be around or toxic for your overall health, then keep your boundaries. The forgiveness can be done at a distance and in the Spirit realm as God wants you to take good care of yourself.

- Learn to talk yourself down on erroneous thoughts. I usually recognize those thoughts because they lead to negative thinking, worry, anxiety, etc. I recognize pretty quickly if I am slipping back into hyperreligious thinking because hyperreligiosity is anchored in performance-based religion contrary to grace-based faith in Jesus. Hyperreligiosity brings conjecture, speculation, worry, and pressure.

- Practice prayer and journaling through a season if you are going through something intense. Write the peaceful life-giving answers down that God gives you that line up with the new covenant of grace and meditate on these answers when problems resurface. The Bible says to cast all our cares on God because he cares for us. The Bible says to be anxious for nothing, but in prayer and supplication to make your requests to the Lord. Then he will give you a peace that surpasses all understanding. The Bible says that God gives them perfect peace who keeps their mind stayed on him. Know that God wants to love on you and remove all heavy burdens. He is gentle, full of love, and grace. You can trust that when you go to him in prayer and in your journal time, his way of doing things will bring peace and healing to your heart and mind. He has taken so many cares off of my mind and replaced it with peace and his reassuring words of an abundant healthy blessed life through Christ Jesus, contrary to my many past erroneous thoughts of self-destructive behavior falsely in his name.

• Know that feelings are not always the truth, and you don't have to be controlled by them. While feelings are important, there is value in sifting through which ones are valid and which ones are destructive and contrary to having a good life that God wants for you. I had extreme feelings in the past and let them rule my mind and behavior. I realize that feelings can sometimes be misleading. As I began to implement healthy behaviors and habits like volunteering, even when my feelings and part of my mind was kicking back, these habits began to stick after time, and I got stronger, began to get back out in life, and formed new beautiful relationships. There is a therapy called cognitive behavior therapy by Dr. Aaron Beck that basically says that your thought life, feelings, and behavior are all interconnected, and if you want to change one of these, it may help to change another. As I began to implement healthy behaviors, my thoughts and feelings eventually caught up and changed in certain areas. I began to come back out of my social shell that I was in after the mental institution stay, and this was one of many tools the Lord provided me with to heal. While I'm not a psychologist, this concept I found to be very useful and informative. On the spiritual side of this equation, I think of the scripture, "We walk by faith and not by sight." Sometimes we think we are inadequate or have timidity, but the Lord wants us to walk in another realm of victory and effectiveness in life. He takes us there gently and with peace guided by the Holy Spirit. In Christ, we can do all things. And with his strength, we can do Christ in all things.

• Be raw and honest before God. God knows your heart, and he just wants you to be you. I used to pray eloquent prayers that I tried to say a certain way. As I grew closer to the Lord, I realized I was his child, and he would rather I say what's on my mind than try to present something a certain way. Yes, there is also power in praying God's Word back to him as you stand on his promises. God loves the sinner and can work with a man or woman who is honest before God than someone in self-righteousness. It is also freeing to know the Father wants to hear what you have to say. No detail is insignificant. If it matters to you, it matters to your loving Father in heaven. When you pray, as Jesus says, believe what you ask for, and if in line with God's will, it will be done. Remember that if you are a believer, God has put favor on your life. Blessings will flow merely because you are bought by the blood of Jesus. As it says in Galatians chapter 3, we are heirs of the promises to Abraham through Christ Jesus. And Abraham was greatly blessed. We are blessed because of a new covenant with God through Jesus that is accessed by faith in Jesus. Sometimes we take for granted the Lord is always working behind the scenes to bless us. As the saying goes, "Count your blessings." He wants to supply all your needs according to his riches in glory by Christ Jesus.

- Though this may be repeating earlier discussions, cast all your cares on God. He can handle anything you bring him and wants to free you of all cares and worry. He will deliver you from any situation or hang-up you have. It may be instant or may occur as he gently leads you to his truth, but you will find healing as you turn to the loving arms of the Father. If you have seen Jesus, as the Bible says, you have seen the Father. Their nature is the same. You can pray to Jesus, the Holy Spirit, or the Father as they are one. They want to hear from you and love you to the point of arms stretched wide on the cross. Jesus bled in the garden of Gethsemane, bled when they put a crown of sharp thorns on his head, bled when his back was torn open by a whip with shards, bled on the cross, bled internally, and bled when they pierced his side at the end. He did this out of love for you and to give you eternal life.

Thank you for reading this book. If this has caused you to think about God or the afterlife, and you want to have 100 percent assurance that when you die, you will go to heaven, know that Jesus died for all your sins—past, present, and future. The Bible says if you will confess him as Lord and believe in your heart he rose from the dead, you will be saved. If you are ready to be saved and have eternal life based on knowing Jesus's sacrifice for you, then pray the following prayer: "Father God in heaven, I thank you for sending your Son Jesus to die on the cross for me. I receive what he did by faith. Jesus, be my Lord. I believe you rose from the dead. Take all my sin upon you. Give me a new heart and life. In Jesus's name. Amen!"

Once again, thanks for reading. Go forward in life. Believe in yourself. Go easy on yourself. No matter what you are going through, there is still hope. Don't give up. Your breakthrough may be just around the corner. Peace and God bless you!

About the Author

Thomas is from Spring, Texas, and grew up the youngest of five siblings. As a child, after watching *Mr. Rogers* on TV, he would go door-to-door and introduce himself to everyone as "neighbor." Perhaps that was a young evangelist in him yet to be discovered. His outgoing personal nature went dormant for a number of years through life's experiences.

After high school, he attended the University of Texas at Austin and majored in civil engineering. After college, he spent seven years as an engineer on the island of Galveston, Texas. After leaving that job, he spent a year attempting to minister for the Lord while also dealing with a mental condition unknown to him at the time that he writes about in his book, *Hyperreligiosity to Grace*.

In the midst of his condition, he attended a two-year Bible school in South Texas and graduated valedictorian. His mental condition continued to cause a number of debilitating setbacks until about four years after Bible school. By the grace of God, he was brought out of a deep valley experience into a new level of understanding of God's love, faithfulness, and restoration to those that have put their trust in Jesus.

He has come out of the pit of mental illness and wants to share with others in his new book what God can do and the future and hope God wants for all of us. He is now happily working again in engineering in Houston, Texas. He enjoys karaoke, writing, reading, antiquing, and studying God's Word. One of his favorite Bible verses is "I can do all things through Christ which strengthens me" (Philippians 4:13). From God's Word and his experience, he believes every person is beautiful and worthy of dignity, healing, and restoration from all life's setbacks.

Lightning Source UK Ltd.
Milton Keynes UK
UKHW051505100223
416597UK00015B/562

9 781685 706517